A World Full of Ghosts

text by **Charis Cotter**   art by **Marc Mongeau**

annick press • toronto + new york + vancouver

We acknowledge the support of the Canada Council for the Arts, the Ontario Arts Council, and the Government of Canada through the Book Publishing Industry Development Program (BPIDP) for our publishing activities.

ONTARIO ARTS COUNCIL
CONSEIL DES ARTS DE L'ONTARIO

Cataloging in Publication

Cotter, Charis
    A world full of ghosts / by Charis Cotter ; art by Marc Mongeau.

ISBN 978-1-55451-182-2 (pbk.).—ISBN 978-1-55451-183-9 (bound)

    1. Ghosts—Juvenile literature.   I. Mongeau, Marc   II. Title.

BF1461.C685 2009   j133.1   C2008-905530-6

The text was typeset in Thicket, designed by Amy Conger, Gill Sans, Animated Gothic Light, and Ratbag.

Distributed in Canada by: Published in the U.S.A. by:
Firefly Books Ltd.   Annick Press (U.S.) Ltd.
66 Leek Crescent   Distributed in the U.S.A. by:
Richmond Hill, ON   Firefly Books (U.S.) Inc.
L4B 1H1   P.O. Box 1338
                                 Ellicott Station
                                 Buffalo, NY 14205

Printed in China.

Visit Annick at: www.annickpress.com
Visit the author at: www.chariscotter.com
Visit the illustrator at: www.marcmongeau.net

For Cate, who is only afraid of the dark.
—C.C.

I have been on a ghost hunt for a few years now and many people have helped me along the way. Robin Cleland, Anita Levin, and Marjory Noganosh have encouraged me to look beneath the surface. Staefan Hannigan took time one wintry day to enchant me with his compelling stories. Thanks also to Heather Benson, Cate Cotter, Graham Cotter, Simon Cotter, Pat Eberle, Stephanie Rowland, Trudy Ruf, and Violeta Uniana, for all your contributions. Emilia Cotter, Julien Procuta, and Julianna Romanyk (my Guinea Piglets) helped with the scariness ratings. The Ontario Arts Council provided a very welcome grant. And a special thanks to my daughter, Zoe, who continues to inspire me with her enthusiastic appreciation of things that go bump in the night.
—C.C.

To Arthur, Rosalie, Matilde, David, and Linda.
—M.M.

Warning To Readers

DON'T READ THIS BOOK:

✗ IN A LONELY, EMPTY HOUSE ALL BY YOURSELF

✗ BY CANDLELIGHT DURING A THUNDERSTORM WHEN THE POWER IS OUT

✗ IN A DARK FOREST UNDER A FULL MOON

✗ ON HALLOWEEN

SCARINESS GUIDE

💀 A little scary

💀💀 Scary

💀💀💀 Very Scary

Contents

Welcome To The World of Ghosts

They live in the creepy-crawly darkness. They lurk in the shadows. They live in trees, in stones, in graveyards. They bark like dogs or roar like lions. Some ghosts like to dance and some like to eat candy. Some bring messages of coming disaster or death and others just want to party all night long.

People all over the world find it deliciously thrilling to sit in the dark telling ghost stories. Although the ghosts may be very different, they all have something in common: they are spirit messengers from another world – the world of the imagination.

So, sit a little closer to the person reading this book. Make sure the lights are on. And get ready to meet some really scary spooks that have been haunting the world for hundreds of years.

France

Ankou the Skeleton

A cold gust of wind, the clatter of a coach and horses, a knock at the door: Ankou (ahn-koo), guardian of the cemetery, has come to collect the dead. Ankou wears a long black cloak and a big hat. His head spins around and around, so he can see everything, everywhere. In France, Ireland, and many parts of Europe, people believe that when Ankou appears, someone will die.

Alaska
Dancing Ahkiyyini

When the ground begins to shake, when the sea rises up in a tidal wave, when boats flip upside down in the water, the Inuit know that Ahkiyyini (ah-ki-yi-nee) is dancing, just for the fun of it. Ahkiyyini, the skeleton ghost, hammers out a frantic rhythm, using his arm as a drumstick and his shoulder blade as a drum. He spins and leaps and stomps his feet as he dances his merry jig across the ice and snow.

The Soldier's Horse

Driving along the road, Philip suddenly swerved the car violently to one side. A huge horse had appeared, looming over the car. Philip could see a man's leg, clad in leather, straddling the horse, and he caught a glimpse of a helmet on the man's head.

"Phew, that was close!" he said to his wife, Ann. "We nearly hit that horse!"

"What horse?" Ann asked.

The road was empty.

They drove around the corner and found themselves at the gates of a grand old estate. That night they learned that the historic house had been the headquarters for the rebels in the English Civil War 350 years before. Philip believes he saw the ghost of a soldier and his horse who had fought in a fierce battle at that site.

—Philip, England

Ireland
The Wailing Banshee

A mournful wailing fills the air. A woman is crying as if her heart will break, but no one can understand a word she says. This is the Irish banshee, who is heard when someone is going to die. Sometimes the banshee is a beautiful woman clothed in a green dress and a gray cloak. Sometimes she is a crooked old crone wrapped in a winding sheet. Her long hair flies out behind her and her eyes are red with weeping.

Jamaica
The Barking Duppy

When a dog's howling and barking can be heard all night, but there is no dog, you can be sure that a duppy (duh-pee) is up to mischief: duppies love to imitate barking dogs. Wicked people who want to use duppies to hurt their enemies call up a duppy by throwing a glass of rum and a few coins on its gravestone. Up jumps the duppy, in a very bad mood, ready to torment the living.

A duppy's breath makes people sick and its touch causes fits. But if a duppy doesn't return to its grave before the sun rises, all its power disappears.

Fireball

One day, when I was about 10, my sister and I were walking up the hill on the way home from school. Suddenly, a huge ball of fire appeared in the road ahead and began rolling towards us. As it gathered speed, it grew bigger and bigger. We stood paralyzed with fear. As it rolled by, a flicker of heat touched our faces. Then we ran home and told our mother, who said it was a duppy.

—*Angela, Jamaica*

Japan
Shojo

Sometimes a Japanese sailor, far out at sea, will catch sight of figures with bright red hair dancing happily on the waves. These are the Shojo (show-jo), the fun-loving sea ghosts who party all day, drinking strong rice wine called sake. Sometimes sailors try to catch the Shojo, luring them to land with a jarful of sake.

Faroe Islands
Sea Ghost

Strange creatures haunt the wild, empty ocean, especially after dark. Fishers from the Faroe Islands sometimes hear blood-curdling screams and howls. Then they spy the Sea Ghost, perched on a small rocky island. The brown creature has only one leg. Or is it a tail? If the fishers are brave enough to let the ghost aboard, it will row with the strength of two men and guide them to the best fishing spots. But as soon as the sun comes up the ghost vanishes into nothing, just as if it were never there.

The Praying Monk

Charles looked around the deserted cathedral. No one in sight. He reached into his coat and pulled out his camera. The janitor had told him no pictures were allowed, but then he'd gone outside, and Charles desperately wanted to take a picture.

A ray of light shone through a lofty stained-glass window, making pretty patterns on the choir stalls. Charles raised the camera to his eye, centered the viewfinder on the empty stalls, and snapped the picture. Satisfied, he put the camera away and then walked up to the altar, enjoying the peace of the quiet, empty church.

Later that month, when Charles had his pictures developed (this was in the days before digital cameras!), he looked eagerly for the picture of the cathedral. There it was, with the ray of sunlight falling on — a man in a hooded monk's robe, kneeling in the choir stalls.

"But there was no one there!" said Charles slowly. He looked closer. Could it be a shadow or a trick of the light? No, it was definitely a monk, his head bent in prayer. Charles had taken a picture of a ghost.

—*Charles, England*

England, Scotland
Silky

A rustle of silk, the glimpse of a long skirt disappearing around a corner, a messy room suddenly tidied up — these are the signs that a silky is living in the house. People consider themselves lucky to be haunted by a helpful silky, who does household chores while everyone is asleep. But if there is a lazy member of the family, the silky will play tricks on him, swirling through his room and tossing all his clothes and toys in the air.

Banks Islands, Vanuatu
Stone Ghosts

People who go walking in the forests on the Banks Islands watch carefully where their shadows fall. One false step and they could be a victim of the stone ghosts, who delight in devouring human souls. These eating ghosts lurk inside large stones, waiting for an unsuspecting person to cross their path. Once the person's shadow touches the stone, the spirits can feast on their prey. But a smart and very careful person can move a stone ghost into their house and keep it there to scare away would-be robbers. When the robbers look through the window, they see the stone ghosts guarding the house and they are afraid to come in. Their shadows might brush the stones and then they would be eaten.

The Woman in the Housedress

Tamieka was alone in her house, doing the laundry in the basement. She hauled a load out of the dryer and started upstairs. As she stepped through the kitchen door, she caught sight of someone standing near the sink. Her heart gave a jump. She knew there was no one else in the house. A second glance revealed a woman with dark brown hair, wearing a flowered housedress, standing over the sink as if she were about to wash the dishes. The woman looked up at her. For a moment their eyes met. Tamieka felt that she knew this woman somehow but couldn't place her. Then the woman was gone and Tamieka was alone in the kitchen.

—*Tamieka, Buffalo*

China

Hungry Ghosts

Blood-red eyes burn in the darkness. An arm stretches out, covered with hairs as sharp as knives. A claw seizes a sweet bun and stuffs it into its mouth. But one bun isn't enough to satisfy this desperate spirit. No matter how much it eats, its huge belly can never be filled. This is an egui, a Hungry Ghost, on the loose during Ghost Month, looking for food and trouble.

Chinese people take good care of their ghostly ancestors: they keep their graves tidy and plant flowers on them, they pray for dead relatives, and they make offerings of delicious food. But the Hungry Ghosts are the lonely souls of people who have no families to pray for them or feed them. They are released into the world for one month only, after the first harvest at the end of July. The living must find ways to protect themselves from these wretched, friendless ghosts.

Monks chant prayers and throw hundreds of buns and sweet candies high in the air. As the offerings tumble towards the earth, the Hungry Ghosts gobble them down, and then children scramble for what's left. At the end of the festival, the Hungry Ghosts burn in a huge bonfire that transports them back to the underworld. A few lucky ones follow floating lanterns down the river to the sea and Buddha's heaven, where they can finally fill their aching stomachs and find peace.

India
Brahmadaitya

The banyan tree, with its thick, spreading branches, makes a perfect climbing tree. But if it is occupied by a Brahmadaitya (brah-mah-die-tya), watch out! This ghost of a long-dead monk hides high in the tree. If anyone dares to climb his tree, the Brahmadaitya makes them fall and break their neck. Otherwise he is a peaceful, rather fussy ghost. He's a very picky eater. The local people bring many different kinds of food, hoping he will find something he likes.

The Dirty Boots

When Joseph was a boy, during the Second World War, he was sent out of Belfast to the country to stay with his Aunt Jane, who had a lovely big house. Aunt Jane was very particular about her housekeeping and didn't like little boys dirtying up the house with their muddy shoes. She drilled it into him that he must take off his outside shoes when he came in from playing in the garden.

Joseph was a little afraid of his Aunt Jane, and he did his best to keep his wet shoes away from her clean floors. But one day he saw the toes of a pair of dirty old boots sticking out from under the long curtains that framed the French doors in the living room. He went and told his aunt not to be mad at him because they weren't his shoes and he didn't know where they came from.

"What are you talking about, child?" asked his aunt, following him into the room.

Joseph pointed to the curtains. The boots were gone but there were muddy footprints on the floor, as if someone had come in from the garden and stood hidden behind the curtains. The footprints were man-sized, so Aunt Jane couldn't blame Joseph. She was quite mystified.

The next day she got a telegram. Her son, Michael, had been killed in action the day before. Joseph and his Aunt Jane both believed that Michael's ghost came back and stood behind the curtains, wearing the muddy boots he had been wearing when he was killed.

—*Joseph, Northern Ireland*

Finland
Liekkio

In the dark of night a sudden dancing flame appears. The liekkio (leek-kee-o) flickers and glows, moving mysteriously through the air and along the ground. There are rumors that long ago a child was killed and secretly buried in the forest. Now its ghost haunts the countryside. Travelers turn their eyes away from the enticing light and hurry home. They know that when the liekkio appears, death soon follows.

Scotland, England
Spunkie

On Halloween night a flight of small white moths flits through the cemetery. They seem to gather around the most recent graves, flickers of white in the darkness. They may look like moths, but these are really the lonely spunkies, ghosts of unbaptized children who died before they could be given names. The spunkies try to follow the spirits of the newly dead to heaven, hoping to sneak in behind them. Sometimes appearing as moths, sometimes as twinkling lights, the sad little spunkies can never find peace.

Ghost Children

My mother went to town one afternoon to do some shopping. It was a hot day and the streets were deserted. As she walked along, she became aware of footsteps following her. She turned and saw a troop of little children scoot around a corner behind her. She began to walk again. Suddenly the children were ahead of her, scurrying down the street. Then they vanished. My mother told me they were ghosts.

—*Jackie, the Philippines*

Jamaica
The Rollin' Calf

Travelers who walk the lonely roads at night may see a giant calf blocking their path. With burning red eyes and a clanking chain around its neck, the Rollin' Calf has a deafening roar. That's how it got its name: in Jamaica, "rollin'" means "roaring." Sometimes the calf takes the shape of a dog or a cat and then grows quickly into a huge horse or a bull. Because the Rollin' Calf loves molasses, it haunts the sugar estates where the sweet, sticky treacle is made. Tradition has it that when a dishonest person dies the bad part of his spirit becomes a Rollin' Calf. There are only two ways to get past this menacing ghost: either threaten it with a whip or wait until the moon comes out and scares it away.

Scotland
Nuggle

On the Shetland Islands, children love to ride the charming little Shetland ponies, which grow no bigger than four feet high. But ancient tradition suggests that there is an even smaller pony, with a lovely tail that curls over its back, lurking in these northern islands. It is the Nuggle, a ghost pony. It is so delightful a creature that people follow it over the hills, hoping to catch it. The mischievous ghost lures them on and on until they reach dangerous water. Then, with a flash of blue light, the Nuggle disappears, leaving its victims teetering on the edge of a cliff or the banks of a rushing river.

Paraguay
Rhea

The Lengua hunters hurry home, casting fearful glances over their shoulders. They are being followed by the distraught ghost of the bird they have just killed. Like an ostrich, the rhea (ree-uh) can't fly, but it can move very quickly across the rough plains. If the rhea's ghost catches up with the hunters it will take its bloody revenge. To fool the ghost, the hunters leave little piles of the dead bird's feathers along the path. Sure enough, the rhea's ghost stops to investigate each pile, looking for the rest of its body. This delays it long enough for the hunters to make it safely back to their village with their dinner.

Ghost Cat

We had two cats: Loki, a white cat, and Bear, a beautiful Siamese. The cats kept their distance and never seemed to get on very well, but when Bear died Loki became very sad. For days, the white cat wouldn't eat and wandered around the house crying.

Bear had his own special cat basket in the family room, near the fire. We washed the blankets to remove Bear's scent and left the basket in its place, hoping Loki might start to use it.

One day, Loki finally approached the basket and stepped gingerly into it. He was just about to settle down when, all of a sudden, he jumped straight up in the air, his fur standing up all over his body, his tail a toilet brush! When he came down to earth, he ran out of the room.

After this, he seemed much happier. He started to eat again and stopped crying. And he went back to the basket. This time he didn't run away but curled up on one side, as if he were making room for another cat beside him. Over the years, Loki continued to use Bear's old basket, always leaving room for Bear's ghost.

—Maria, San Francisco

Gabon, Africa
Awiri

In Gabon, West Africa, the ancestors linger long after they die, watching over their descendants and protecting them from evil. The white awiri (ah-weary) are seldom seen, but their relatives can feel their guardian presence. When they walk in the wild places – on a high mountain, beside a lake or a river, or past a huge rock or a tall tree – they walk silently, because they know the awiri are close by. They leave little offerings for the elusive ghosts: pretty stones, a few delicate shells, or some colorful leaves arranged in a pattern.

Hawaii
Aumakua

In Hawaii, the ghost gods are everywhere: in the trees, the roaring wind, the mighty volcanoes, and the pounding waves of the sea. The aumakua (ow-mah-koo-ah) watch over their descendants and help them whenever they can. When the crops are dry the aumakua inhabit the clouds and bring rain. If a tame shark appears that likes to have its head rubbed, you can be sure that's an aumakua come to visit a relative.

A Visit From Granddad

When Kerry was a little boy, he looked up the staircase one day and saw his grandfather, dressed in black, walking across the hall from one of the bedrooms to the bathroom.

Kerry went into the kitchen and said to his mother, "What's Granddad doing here?"

"Granddad's not here," said his mother, busy with the cooking. "He's at his house in Belfast." Belfast was twenty miles away.

Later that evening a relative called with some sad news. Kerry's grandfather had died that afternoon, just about the same time the boy saw him crossing the hall.

—Kerry, Northern Ireland

Mexico
The Day of the Dead

The cemetery is lit up with candles and torches. Picnic baskets overflow with delicious food, arches of bright marigolds tower over the gravestones, grinning toy skulls and skeletons are propped up against photographs of dead people. Children play tag and grown-ups laugh and sing. It's party time in the cemetery, Mexico's favorite holiday: Día de los Muertos, the Day of the Dead.

On this one day of the year, death is something to laugh at and no one is afraid. People come to the cemetery to celebrate life and death with their favorite ghosts. The children eat sugar skulls and Bread of the Dead. The sounds of their merrymaking rise up and float in the air. The pain of death is forgotten and everyone is happy.

The Lady in White

Sasha and Mina were having a sleepover. They were on the fold-out couch in the basement and they stayed up late, talking. Finally they feel asleep. Deep in the darkest time of the night, Sasha woke up. A white figure stood above the bed, looking down on her. At first she thought it was Mina's mother, but as she looked closer she saw that it couldn't be, because Mrs. Solomon had short, dark hair, and this was a woman with long blonde curls. She wore a long white dress trimmed with lace.

"You're a ghost, aren't you?" whispered Sasha. The figure stared at her.

Sasha closed her eyes tightly and then opened them again. The white lady was still there.

"Thank you for coming," said Sasha. "I've always wanted to see a ghost." Then she smiled at the lady and went back to sleep.

—*Sasha, Toronto*

North America
Navajo Chindi

A whistling in the dark. A shadow that moves stealthily just beyond the light. The rustling of wind moving through dead leaves – but there is no wind and there are no leaves. These are all signs of the presence of a chindi (chin-dee), the ghost that rises up from the last dying breath of a Navajo. The Navajo believe that within every person there is both good and evil. When a person dies, the good and evil are separated. The good spirit passes into the Navajo underworld, but the bad spirit is released into the world. If a Navajo dies inside her house, her relatives remove the corpse, seal up the doors and windows, and go away. The evil chindi will haunt the house forever.

Saudi Arabia
Afrit

A swirl of smoke rises from a body on the ground. A man has been murdered, and a ghost is created from his spilled blood. The Arabian afrit (a-freet) is an angry spirit that seeks revenge. If someone thinks fast and drives a nail into the pool of blood, the afrit will not form. But if no one nails down the ghost, a dangerous afrit will rise into the air and pursue the murderer to punish him.

The Shoe Factory

Werner was visiting his friend Peter, who had just bought an old building and was planning to fix it up so he could live in it. Werner spent some time looking around.

"Well, what do you think of it?" Peter asked him.

"Very nice, but a bit crowded, don't you think?" answered Werner.

"Crowded? There's no one here."

"I saw a man and a woman working on the third floor, along with a few other people."

This is what Werner saw: a stooped, gray-haired man in a brown leather apron bent over a woman who was sitting at a table, working on a shoe. The man was checking her work. In the background, the other people were all working on shoes. The women wore long skirts. Werner believes he had a glimpse into the building's past, when it was a shoe factory. He had seen the ghosts of workers from a hundred years before.

—Werner, Germany

West Africa
Ibambo

The forest is still at night. Nothing moves. A man hurries along a lonely path, wishing he were safe at home. Suddenly, from the corner of his eye, he sees a white shape appear from behind a tree. He turns – and the figure vanishes. He picks up his pace, his heart in his throat. Suddenly the ibambo (i-bam-bo) is there again, on his other side this time. It seems to glide silently from tree to tree. The man begins to sweat. He never should have risked the path at night. Everyone knows the ibambo lurk in the shadowy darkness. These mysterious spirits of the dead seem to delight in staying just out of sight. The man breaks into a run, but the ibambo is always there, mocking him. By the time he finally gets home he is half-mad with fear, quivering, and talking wildly about the ghost in the forest. His family members look at each other. "Ibambo," they say.

Japan
The Legless Yurei

As the clock strikes two in the morning the wind stirs in the trees. A dim figure appears, floating above the ground. Two purple flames burn steadily, one on either side of it. Tall, with disheveled black hair flowing down over its shoulders, the yurei (you-ray) glides through the garden toward the house where it once dwelt. A long white kimono trails behind it, almost hiding the fact that it has neither legs nor feet. The yurei is caught between the world of the dead and the world of the living, seeking revenge from those who harmed it in life.

The Man in the Hat

Ned woke up. A figure wearing a dark coat and an old-fashioned hat with a brim stood in the doorway. Ned sat up and stared. He was about to ask the man who he was when he noticed the figure had no legs. Then it slowly disappeared, dissolving into nothing.

A few weeks later, Ned heard his little boy, Geoffrey, talking to someone upstairs. Geoffrey was three. Ned asked Geoffrey whom he had been talking to. "The man in the hat," said Geoffrey.

One month later, Ned's wife, Alice, was making their bed. She turned and saw a man standing behind her, wearing a dark coat and hat. "Go away, right now!" said Alice. The man disappeared and was never seen again. But Ned did some research and discovered that a man had lived in their house for thirty years. He was a businessman who worked in the city at a time when men always wore wide-brimmed hats to work. The man had died in that bedroom fifty years before Ned and Alice moved in.

—Ned, Boston

Hawaii
Lapu

Misty shapes hover above the crumbling temple ruins, and the faint sounds of drumming and chanting float upon the air. A troop of ghosts sweeps down a deserted roadway, dancing and playing as the spirits follow a long-forgotten path. The lapu (lah-poo) are doomed to wander, never finding any rest. In life, they were desperate outcasts with no home, no family, and no friends. In death, they lurk in dark places, looking for butterflies and spiders to eat, because no one ever brings them offerings of food. Sometimes they leap from cliffs into the western sea, hoping to reach Milu, the underworld that lies deep beneath the ocean waves.

Argentina
The Wandering Gaucho

The vast, grassy plains – the pampas – stretch endlessly from east to west. Occasionally, herds of cattle will move slowly through, accompanied by a gaucho (gow-cho) and his horse. It's a lonely life, and a hard one. Many a gaucho tells the story of seeing a ghost out there in the pampas: a cowboy in a brightly woven poncho, riding his horse. This ghost might have been a real person once, but most likely the tale is a legend passed down through many generations. Long ago, a gaucho became obsessed with weaving the most beautiful poncho in the world. He worked on it night and day, neglecting his cattle and his family. Finally he finished it and rode to a fiesta to show off his wonderful creation. But a giant bird swept down and killed him, and for his pride he was doomed to wander the pampas until the end of time.

The Lady in the Cemetery

When we were six, my friends and I liked to hide in the bushes on the hill beside the cemetery, telling secrets. Beyond the iron fence the tombstones marched in rows, over-grown with vines and long grass.

One day as we sat there we saw a woman walking along the line of gravestones. She was small, with neat gray hair done up in a bun. Her face was lined but her fine skin was pale and creamy. She wore flat shoes and a long navy-blue coat. The coat was covered with big moons and bright, silvery stars.

As she walked along she mumbled to herself. I couldn't make out what she was saying. We all watched her silently. As she got to the end of the line of stones she turned and looked at us.

"I can't find it," she said. She looked so sad. "I can't find it!" she said again. She looked straight at us with her mournful eyes and we couldn't stand it anymore. We all jumped up and ran home.

Later, I thought about it. I think she was a lost ghost, looking for her grave.

—*Keisha, Chicago*

North America
Halloween

Hundreds of years ago, a huge bonfire burned on a hilltop in Ireland. People dressed in wild costumes and masks, hoping to fool the evil spirits who lurked just outside the light from the fire. They were celebrating Samhain, an ancient Celtic festival. Over the centuries, the Samhain traditions became mixed in with two Christian holidays: All Saints'

Day (All Hallows) on November 1 and All Souls' Day on November 2. People remembered the dead on All Souls' Day and went door to door, begging for little buns called soul cakes. Eventually October 31 – All Hallows Eve – became our Halloween.

Nowadays, sugar and spooks go hand in hand as people dress up in costume, decorate their houses, and hand out sweet treats to children. Spiderwebs, grinning jack-o-lanterns, flying bats, and mock grave-yards transform friendly neighborhoods into horrible haunts. All sorts of monsters, ghosts, and strange characters walk the streets, asking for candy. Are they all kids? Or are some of them real ghosts, escaped from the graveyard for one night to have fun and eat little chocolate bars?

The Back Bedroom

When I was about ten, our family moved to a rambling old house in the country.

The house had three bedrooms. My parents painted the two front bedrooms, and they were very pleasant. But the back bedroom had a funny, cold feeling about it. It was a sunny room, and there was no reason for it to be cold. It also smelled odd, and no amount of airing out or air freshener seemed to help.

Nobody wanted to be in that room so it was left until last to fix up. Eventually, we did paint it, and all the doorknobs and window latches were removed, cleaned and polished, and put back securely.

My sister was away at college and didn't know how we felt about the back bedroom. But, when she came home, she reacted the same way to that room. Then her boyfriend came to visit, and he was put in the "guest room," with absolutely nothing said about any of this history.

All seemed well until the doorknob came off in his hand. He yelled for help, but nobody could hear him because the walls were so thick. Eventually he got out (I don't remember how), but he was so scared and upset he went home right away, and that was the end of him as a boyfriend.

After all of these events, my parents heard a story from the neighbors. It seems that old Mrs. Forester had lived there for many years with her unmarried son, Jimmy, described by all as a real gentleman. When old Mrs. Forester died, Jimmy went on living there alone for some years. But it seems that Jimmy had a secret: when he was alone he drank heavily. When the neighbors hadn't seen him for a few days, they broke into the house. They found him in his room, dead.

The back bedroom that nobody liked was Jimmy's room.

—Marianne, Ithaca